MOTHERS OVER NANGARHAR

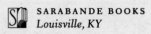

SARABANDE BOOKS
Louisville, KY

PAMELA HART

MOTHERS

OVER

NANGARHAR

Library of Congress Cataloging-in-Publication Data
Names: Hart, Pamela, author.
Title: Mothers over Nangarhar : poems / Pamela Hart.
Description: First edition. | Louisville, KY : Sarabande Books, 2018.
Identifiers: LCCN 2017058703 (print) | LCCN 2017059930 (e-book)
ISBN 9781946448279 (e-book) | ISBN 9781946448262 (pbk. : acid-free paper)
Classification: LCC PS3608.A7866 (e-book) | LCC PS3608.A7866 A6 2018 (print)
DDC 811/.6—DC23
LC record available at https://lccn.loc.gov/2017058703

Cover and interior design by Alban Fischer.
Cover image © prill/iStock
Manufactured in Canada.
This book is printed on acid-free paper.
Sarabande Books is a nonprofit literary organization.

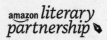

This project is supported in part by an award from the National Endowment for the Arts.
The Kentucky Arts Council, the state arts agency, supports Sarabande Books with
state tax dollars and federal funding from the National Endowment for the Arts.

FOR MY FAMILY

Arriving from always, you'll go away everywhere

—RIMBAUD

CONTENTS

V

INTRODUCTION

A poem, by its very nature, is an ancillary and obsessive thing. Were the state a ship, as Horace put it to us in his odes, then a poem, political or not, would be the wake of that ship, impossible without it, doggedly pursuing it—a thing apart and yet integral. To live a life without poetry is to look out from the ship on which we cross the short sea of our existence and see the water unmoved, untroubled, untouched, and to think nothing of it, the sea slick and without sound. No one would ever confuse a ship with the parting water that pursues it, and yet a ship without its wake, like a wake without its ship, would be a ghost ship, a sign of death-in-life, a form of terror.

Mothers Over Nangarhar speaks back to the world while being deeply aware of its own nature in this wakeful way, aware of the strange and haunting paradox of having given life to the world that encircles it and having also been brought to life by that same world, the paradox of being in the middle of a war without being on the ground, the imagination brimming in the wake of the ship of state. The book circles its subject with the poignant uncertainty of whether it is merely observing or being dragged down into the depths. These are poems that move like liquid, pursuing what has been lost in those distanced decisions as life turned a corner and bent out of sight, that move with a foreboding sense of an approaching but unconfirmed shipwreck, having passed cindered flotsam in the sand.

The deft use of craft in *Mothers Over Nangarhar*, with its admirable range of influence, allusion, and form, doesn't paper over the collection's sense of its own ancillary and obsessive nature. At its heart this book is a story of the mother's mind making sense of a child tossed overboard and into the jaws of war. How does the mind make sense of this—the nightmare of your child being chewed and spat out by Scylla and Charybdis and then sent back to you? How does the body make sense of this—by seeking communion with nature and art and others, or through the search for virtual knowledge?

Somewhere between theory and therapy but free of the constraints of both, *Mothers Over Nangarhar* moves through its mazy, crazed world of intimate and global conflict, exterior and interior pain, searching and assured. It is a beautiful, strong, and vulnerable work for our beautiful, strong, and increasingly vulnerable world.

—Rowan Ricardo Phillips

June 2017

MOTHERS OVER NANGARHAR

WAR PARTITA

Dear one

From the yard I see Mars

While you keep watch in far-off deserts

I check the world clock

Looking for the force of cluster

I recon the conflict

Secure the day's perimeter

Tripwire my better angels

Oh you of frenzied armor

Carve this song

Into your bullet

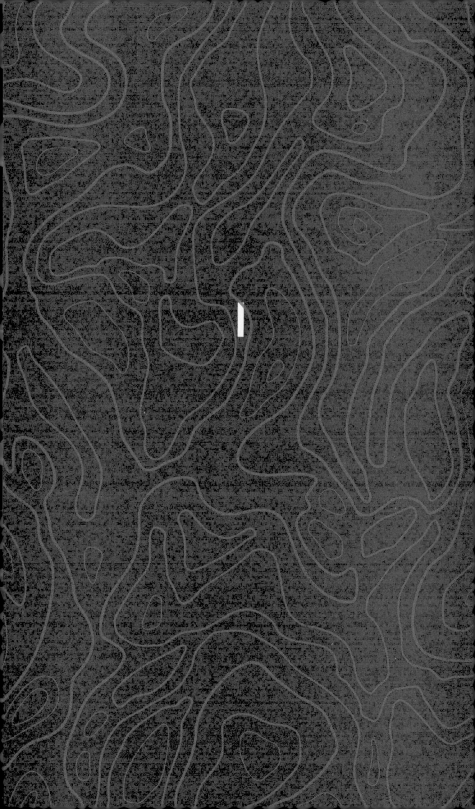

CITIES & SIGNS & WAR

If all cities are Venice and all Venice is memory then where will you be deployed. Will you see Venice in Kabul. Their architectures spreading across arid plain and narrow canal. There you go. You may walk and walk and not notice anything real and when you do see something maybe you'll know that thing as a sign of another thing. Here you are. Your M4 over your shoulder. Marco Polo tells Khan the streets are written pages; the city says everything. But you are reading an unruly discourse. It may have nothing or everything to do with the city of your deployment. Your face burns as it hunts. The signs are signs of other things. What do I as your mother know of this. Nothing.

RIVER OF PAINTED ROCKS

Along the Chattahoochee we walk. Men fish in its muddy shoals. Also cormorants. Pelicans sun in a river of painted rocks. I'm proud. It's the marching. The uniform. The order. Heat oozes. Fish break the cinnamon surface. I notice your eyelashes. How dark. You were a blond baby. Now you are a soldier. You have an Adam's apple I see. Your skin is clear. I hear my father saying your skin is clear. I talk to him for a very long time in the parking lot of the Red Barn Restaurant. It's our last lunch. I don't know this then. See how the mind is torn from topic to topic. We don't visit Carson McCullers's home. She married a soldier from Fort Benning. Its stucco houses, the red-tiled roofs. You liked to paint. You were not an artist. There's no rushing mountain stream to this story.

WAR GAMES

In a photograph posted online plastic soldiers crouch behind switchbacks of sand and twigs. Several lie sideways in the dirt, like helpless turtles. Miniature paper flags flutter near the enemy's berm. Elsewhere a mustard-yellow cowboy idles, his hat hanging off the back of his head as the pistol is fired. His target is decked out in headdress and chaps, rifle in one hand and bow in the other. My son's first gun was a dinosaur.

FLYNN'S POND

My pregnant belly
your small torso
below the pond's skin
us drifting
in an overcast day
the pond itself floating
like a ceramic boat
in the middle of the world
surfaces unmarked by breeze
or the scar of us
the water's desire for our bodies
our want for its glassy touch
you're safe said the pond
its blanket
coiling around our legs

TO THE PERSON WHO ASKED ABOUT NEGOTIATING DIFFERING PERSPECTIVES WITH MY SON IF THERE ARE ANY WHILE SUPPORTING HIS CHOICE

In the video he stands at the plastic yellow-and-blue easel

A big sheet of paper is covered with slashes and drips

His awkward grip on the brush

Our old dog lumbering into the scene

Dog and boy hug

Keep going I say

Cars splash through melting

snow on pavement

Drip drip goes

the gutter

Can I stop he asks

Back then I did not see how morning made us

We moved unevenly through the day

filling it with fine motor skills and bad food

I did not recognize that paint on paper

one winter afternoon

would be anything more

than what it was which was

that he didn't finish

and the dog wandered

out of the frame

AT THE SHOOTING RANGE

Shell casings ricochet off my arm
    flicker like hummingbirds

Hot from flight they snag
    in the weave of my sweater

Such beautiful moltings and scatterlings
    these brassy hearts

The gun's barrel is domestic gray
    like a pen in my hand

To know what you know I load
    seventeen hollow-point

bullets to nest
    in the chamber

I squeeze the trigger of the spring-loaded frame
    as one shot a thousand feet

per second flies toward the target
    its jolt tangling my hair

WOMEN & WAR SESTINA

We pass around Jane's photo
In black & white a helmet
covers her soldier's face
Somewhere in Afghanistan there's news
We complain that we don't know
how things are going

I worry about my son's going
& stroke the edges of Jane's photo
Like a charm, it shields my knowing
the specifics of his helmet
I guard against too much news
but headlines mark my face

Every war zone is a face
scarred by combat's goings
Jane anticipates bad news
wonders if unevenness in the photo
means her soldier's tilted helmet
is a sign of unknown knowns

Mary panics that she doesn't know
Searches blurry images for faces
& declares history like a helmet
sings with soldiers' going
I notice how light in Jane's photo
slants in shadows across some news

We're good at dodging news
Can't be hurt by what we don't know
Secretly I stare at the photo
even as lines in my face
recur like prayers against going
My words airborne like helmets

The story of soldiers' helmets
marks the headlined news
that war is fed by comings & goings
of the sons & daughters we know
How we ache to hold their faces
when looking at Jane's photo

Face the facts, we sing
while knowing soldiers' photographs
behold their ever-goingness

THE CUT

The day after I sliced off my fingertip, I got up before anyone to finish trimming the plant's woody stems. This time I cut the pepper berries with pruning shears, arranged them in a vase. Later in the kitchen the work went on around me. My husband chopped onions. One son peeled apples and said how do you use this dull thing. My daughter measured flour and butter for the crust. The other son stayed asleep and did not set the table. I watched them slip into my form, take on an aspect of me and how that happens when some part goes missing. This was like happiness. How they hurried to fill the cut. How they stitched together the slight emptiness.

IN THE RED CROSS PARKING LOT
AFTER A MEETING ON PTSD

What about your son, Kathy
wonders but really

she wants to talk about her son
Tim in Afghanistan

who never got with the program
six-two, on the baseball team

kicked out of high
school, has trouble with rules

which is how she explains
his wild streak, there's his hat

on the dashboard
Tim, she insists

won't make a career of this
As her hand brushes the dark

spotlights halo the white-domed
rescue vehicles around us

Next door someone shouts
Further off traffic continues

along the expressway. Kathy
sends care packages, the good

socks, knows where to get them
The rifle bolt she bought him—

it's expensive, doesn't jam or clog
Tim's sergeant killed, when will Tim

get with the program, her words
rocketing on in the night

Like the Spartan women, we polish
our sons in the concrete firmament

SOMETIMES WE TALK ABOUT NOTHING

Her son's platoon
is moving
to a dangerous place

At the market Beth says
the strawberries
are huge

So sweet she eats
some
every day

And wonders will
she hear
from him soon

I picture the red
fruit its juice
pooling

THE SHAWL

Threaded with silver and gold
it flickered in the meeting

room's fluorescence
Marie wrapped the fabric

around her neck
as if in Kabul's embrace

She wanted what silk knows
when it changes color

and refracts incoming light
how it curls into a ball

when it burns
We touched it too

as if it had been worn
by our soldier

LANDAYS FOR ALAHA

Dear one, at the museum we looked
through glass at blue calligraphy

Gilded pages of *The Bird Conference*
confined in well-lit cases

Consider the hoopoe, its needled
beak meddling with history

Your father explains Persian
is Farsi is Dari isn't Pashto

Rumor has it the crows
of Khost have gone mad

Dreaming of my son I fly to your
country but the plane cannot land

When night was a hoopoe
it seized your father's heart

Later the heart said
I'm tired of America

I apologize—feathers drift
from my mouth like ribbons of war

My syntax breaks to lake ice
Who am I to translate the exodus of birds

THE MATINS PROJECT

The moon shoves its silver into my left eye
even as it departs

In morning's gray I become lake
then witch, and drink the silky water

Clouds collect above tree lines
while my worry list snarls the bed covers

Picasso said he painted to stop motion
Tell that to another five minutes gone

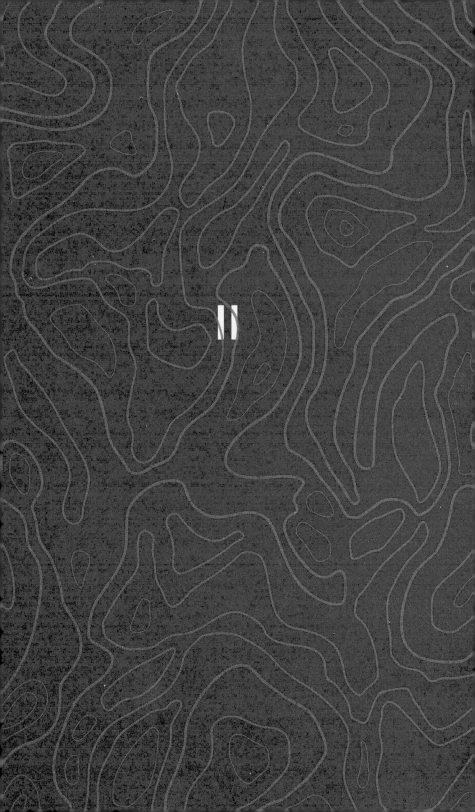

THE WOMEN

Joanie tells us she's
not good at talking
when he's home on leave
I'm getting married Stella announces
the dress is all picked out
You don't want to baby him
Should I get his favorite food
Maybe wait to buy the dress
Our words weaving
in and out of the metal chairs
He was such a punk
The Marines were good
for him says Mary
Jane wants a do-over
It's like being married to a stranger
I don't want to fight anymore
It's hard to listen
to people Shelly says
We count the days
check the inbox
We unspool our biggest
dread and make
it into a beautiful spider

GRACE WATCHES THE NEWS
AND IS UNABLE TO SLEEP

Tonight it's two soldiers
killed by a roadside bomb

I say knowledge is an amulet
But Grace complains her bones ache

Either way, I read history
to ward off unknowns

Grace explains her daughter's
in Kandahar or maybe Herat

Truck lights wash my windshield
on the way home

Losing track I read the signs
Sun Tzu describes

four constellations
When the moon

is in Sagittarius
the winds rise

I keep scanning the air
waves for more

DURING WAR WE EMAIL OUR SOLDIERS

We thought *The Gates* created
A sense of tension
With Central Park
Your father calls them saffron
I say they're orange
How are things

                       Living conditions are fine. I have my own room
                              The Army makes Kirkuk
                                   seem like Iowa

The sun was out
Your mother and I walked
The blue sky dazzled
& white snow
Trivial from where you are
Check the news all the time
We haven't heard much

               Showers broken /no hot water/ but thankful for the fact
                            there actually are showers

Such a long time since I've written
Sorry! Think of you always
Generally better at mailing
Packages than writing

Hi Daddy
I'm busy. Keeping out of trouble
Just letting you know no news from here

CONTOUR DRAWING

To make a contour drawing do not look at the paper. Focus on the object. Position your pencil and do not lift it again. Begin by marking an imaginary line. Hand and pencil mimic the form. Look closely. What if I make a contour drawing of my son's head. Hair shaved to the skull. Its shape sharp against the backdrop of wall or sky. Or the infant's head. Or head on a pillow. Head wearing the striped baseball cap of a boy. Keep looking. My pencil working its way into the story of a son.

MUSEUM

We visit the Hirshhorn. Bourgeois's spiders and ominous glass constructions consume us. Next, the Holocaust Museum. All the shoes, the Tower of Faces. How to curate the dead. At the Air and Space Museum we sit in a lunar capsule. Words flit around us. I consider a museum of language. Diagrammed sentences throughout the garden like massive di Suvero sculptures. Site-specific collaged etymologies installed in the atrium. We joke about a museum of lies. Falsehoods with explanatory wall text. Misstatements and denials near the escalator. Later my son packs for boot camp.

LAND NAVIGATION

Lately the mother believes in the concept of the map. She remembers the stack on a seat of the family wagon as it rumbled cross-country. Now as she holds an unfolded grid of blue and red lines she pictures what's ahead. For instance, the map of Afghanistan. How the topography moves is hard to pin down. She's not good with details. Night vision goggles would be useful. Measure the coordinates. Point A when the son first mentions the Army to Point B. Which is when will he leave and where will he go. Slow the racing sentences. Study gradient points. The associative mind is restless. Language is fickle.

IN THE CAR

Jack talks about Afghanistan
I say I've never been in a Corvette

Like a sea creature the Big
Dipper floats above us

The night an inverted wave
stars dipped in phosphorescence

air splashing
in the front seat

Jack leans into a curve
and downshifts

along the narrow blacktop
Cornfields blur

at 110 miles per hour
The sky shivers, cracks

I love him and loathe him
like his mother

like an ocean I carry
his broken parts

NUMEROUS GRAY AREAS

For Paula Loyd, US Army Human Terrain System

Mapping the flat
earth of soldiers

I note the border
between dune and bomb

I gather artifacts of custom
to translate for my soldiers

The right hand for eating
soles of feet turned from faces

Swimming into the war zone
I collect gossip like seashells

Say good anthropology
makes for better killing

While meadowing I'm ethnographer
counterintelligence of the cooking pot

Now I am a column of fire
dark outline at the center

Hear the crackle and hiss of my body
my voice calling their names

PRAISE SONG

A morning prayer to all
That keeps you safe

To body armor and weapons
The drill sergeant and the bullet

Interpreter and phrase book
To MREs and rocket launchers

Also the forward operating
Base and your radio operator

The helicopter pilots and soldiers
Who donate blood the medic

And tourniquet
Dog tags and helmet

I sing of your boots caked
In clay rough with hours

Of the IED you don't step
On and the dog who finds it

The specialist and sniper
Tip of the spear and rear guard

I want to praise the desert
The women of Afghanistan

Tajik Pashtun Hazara
May they be wild with fury

To your smile
And your instinct

A praise song to next month and the next
Each one bringing you home alive

LOOKING AT MONET'S *WATER LILIES*

After Robert Hayden

When my son was downrange
    I wanted to be lost
in an onrush of lavender
    to be missing among green
as Monet's light dissolved to magenta
    Even as the crush of the crowd
shattered my faith in iridescence
    even as the room divided into
flower and vowel
    I would sit in the corner
where the blue endured
    where my son
had become beautiful and dangerous

ON THE ORANGE JUMPSUIT

In the LiveLeak image James Foley blinks in the desert sun.

His orange jumpsuit shimmers. It's wrong to watch
      but the orange is exuberant.
Christo called it saffron.

A table of pashmina shawls in the plaza
      under blossoming pear trees.
Especially delicious is the orange one

a counterpoint to my habit of blue.

Mohamedou Ould Slahi in Cuba.
      "I was wrapped in Afghani cloths."
Guantánamo procedures include

cutting away
      old uniforms
and issuing the orange garb.

James Foley is signaling a message in Morse code, I decide.
      It's defiance, not fear. Orange means gluttony.
Also the second chakra. Also amusement and poison.

Van Gogh searched for orange, hoping it would "harmonize the
    brutality of extremes."

Jumpsuits come in hot pink, yellow, lime green,
    navy, khaki, chocolate brown, gray, and high-security orange.
There are matching socks. Bob Barker, not the game show host,

started his prison supply business in the 1970s.
    First he sold slushy machines. Now it's color-coded
handcuffs. I don't know how to write that poem.

It must be the sun, though it's a myth women blink more
    than men. James Foley's mouth is a slash in the sky.
We blink 29,000 times a day. I pause the video to see if there's a pattern.

I click and count, telling no one.
The video disappears from the site.

The next time I notice James Foley's forehead
    how the large vein called the
supratrochlear strains against skin. I'm also watching

Chicago Fire and this week someone is being extricated
    from a burning car. Or building.
Maybe someone is about to jump.

I haven't worn the orange pashmina in years and it's probably
not made from the wool of a Himalayan mountain goat.

"Life was suddenly blown into ███████,"
    writes Mohamedou Ould Slahi. I picture orange
uniforms shattering in a prison yard.

"Dance the orange," said Rilke about the fruit not the color
    but really he was thinking of death. The marigold is called
flor del muerto, flower of the dead. What about the blood orange.

When news of Steven Sotloff's beheading comes in the fall
    I watch the video. He's kneeling in a rocky
landscape that offsets his orange.

I think of Rilke's instruction and how the color
fights, drowning itself in its own taste.

Later there are jumpsuits everywhere. Even the double yellow line
    looks orange as I drive. Bulletins about
David Haines and the pilot in the cage.

Children depicted in a protest photo.
The line of orange men walking on a beach.

The history of orange is about a word
    that begins in Sanskrit as *nāranga-s*, flows to
Persian *nārang* and into Arabic as *nāranj*

then to old French
    where the *n* disappears along a riverbank
snagged by a willow root.

In England the fruit arrives before the color
    which is called yellow-red until the 16th century.
And there's no true rhyme.

It's true we give in to distraction
        as if it's a murderer
there, waiting to kill.

In Jordan they give Mohamedou Ould Slahi
        a blue outfit.
Uniforms, he says, represent backward and communist countries.

The pashmina's glow, Slahi's diary, the news,
        the sky over a snowfield at dusk,
my eyes track the orange, meandering

like Christo's panels, installed in 2005 as Slahi flows into his third year
        of detention.

You don't own your jumpsuit no matter the color
        and it's really not like stepping into the same river,
jumpsuits rushing their orange through history.

I find it difficult
        to stop thinking
about James Foley.

To stop looking—
        Is that to let go.

MY SOLDIER

At Mount Vernon they manage lines. Here's one snaking through the house, library and dining room. Up to the low-ceilinged bedrooms. Down to kitchen and pantry, along the back stairway to the outside, where it is March and warm above the Potomac River. I am looking back now. I am writing backward to figure out forward. Gesturing behind to describe what's approaching. This May morning the early fog rises and dissipates over the pond. That March afternoon I stand with my son in a line that moves in an orderly fashion. The breeze moves in the line too, following us into the house, listening as a guide explains colors in the dining room. It is and is not the same breeze that annoyed Mr. Washington in March is something I consider while looking at unruly May greens chattering in the trees. I'm not good with plot. I fiddle with the shape of these lines. One morning my son gets in line and there are other soldiers with him.

WAR STORIES

Stories of war begin midsentence is one way to start. This isn't a story of war. This is the mother on the idea of a son at war. Can he kill is a story. Will the mother blame herself could be another. And how does the mother feel. The mother doesn't like that word. The mother likes the word think. Will ideas versus feelings get in the way. Is this the story of mothers of soldiers. The mothers' lives are windy. The air is elastic. The story is a story on the idea of war and the son who might kill or be killed. She could or could not change this.

BIRDS RISING ARE A SIGN OF AMBUSH

Here's that dream about the party. We're at Fort Benning. The dining room is framed by rafters in a cathedral ceiling. Chairs and people come and go. An old rotary phone rings. It's aunt so-and-so. The feng shui, she says, is wrong. Someone, she says, has died. Off we go in her red car. It crashes into a boulder. No one is hurt. Chapter two. A friend arrives with bags from Bed Bath & Beyond. The husband who looks like an army officer isn't happy. The friend runs into the road. The screech of car wheels. The end. I awaken. It's still dark. I take the dog out. Cicadas are drumming. It's almost fall despite the humidity. The fray, says Sun Tzu, can bring gain; it can bring danger.

NIGHT VISION

There's not much evidence the War
      of 1812 was fought nearby as beer
and music pulse Fridays at the Anchor

The men all close cut and right
      postured loudly in your face
young women with their jeans

pressed tight hair skinny and long
      like the night bearing down
No sign in the mirror of shot glasses

clattering in clutches along tall
      tables where "Uncle John's Band"
clashes with Katy Perry's "Roar"

It's the end of the drinking
      season the war
bar filled with tourists and soldiers

tales spilling from tattoos and vodka
      what they know almost lost
in the hazy crush of sweat and sound

Night circles possibility
      and regret
You listen to the army wife

talking about her brother
        dead of cystic fibrosis
the lieutenant who can't sleep

Pearl who owns the place loves these guys
        gives you a free round
says her cancer is good for now

You know how it goes
        Imagination
will be your enemy and lover

The war children will dance
        their words beating
across the great river

that continues outside
        night falling
into your mouth all of it

MOTHERS OVER NANGARHAR

Powered by search engines
     and history
mothers navigate

Google Earth, view the flashing
     lights of MRAPs
as the cursors flag river or range

The mothers leap across time zones
     check their satellite feed
sprint from screen to field

where you lie
     split
calling their name

The mothers fly from Fallujah
     Wanat, Khe Sanh to Marathon
Hastings, Vicksburg

Their hands are epic
     their bodies large pouring
into and out of you

DRONE SONG

By lake lapping I hear it
    Across wadi and village
The startling
    As it skims
An empire of hum
    Against my arm
Like a dragonfly I say
    To skyscraper and avenue
Picture Yemeni blue
    Afternoon light
        Is a seedpod I say to no one in particular
Because the glossy abelia
    Is nearly in bloom
        The scream of matter everywhere
Ready to strike

PRIVATE JONATHAN LEE GIFFORD'S MOTHER

Because she thinks about him every day
Remembers when he started kindergarten
That he always called her at the first snowfall
Because the knock on the door the night
She learned he'd been killed
She says she doesn't concern herself
With thoughts about the cost of the war
Because there are days she sits in her kitchen
Turning the blender on and off

KEVLAR POEM

The woman who invented Kevlar
liked to walk in the woods with her father
naming trees and plants
She collected leaves
to press and save
She sketched the sky and fern beds
the rocks along streams
The woman who discovered Kevlar
liked to sew clothing for her dolls
thought she might be a fashion designer
Her father died when she was ten
and there was no Kevlar for heart disease
or her sadness
The woman who discovered
Kevlar loved the messy
astonishing world
She contemplated chemicals
while spinning strands
of a polymer brew
to concoct
something synthetic and strong
fine enough to be woven
into the reed of a woodwind instrument
or the panel of a bulletproof vest

REGARDING THE IMPROVISED EXPLOSIVE DEVICE

If this poem had wires coming out of it,
you would call the words devices.

—KEVIN POWERS

And then, click, the blast
      a pyrotechnic spectacle
of fertilizer and chemical
      geysering
into a scroll of smoke and sand
      I begin by imagining the soldier's form
launched into a falling tree
      parts of him smoldering in Kandahar

Because there's no narrative I decide to make
      a ghost heart
by stitching memory to picture
      the afterimage
of his phantom arms material enough

It's important to know that from Benghazi
      to Belfast the devices tend to be homemade
a brew of toolbox or kitchen implements
      exploding like paint
colors shattering the militant air

If drawing were my thing, I'd sketch the valley's
      bowl of stars, describe a woman waking
to step into Kandahar's chill

But what's the point of form
if it can't devise a way to
            find the hidden wire

Alternately I read about the soldier
            who could be but isn't mine
And let's say I decide to think about
            mayflies spinning
in a narrow bar of afternoon
            the trout camouflaged by stone
Let's say the wires touch

or that I'm some soldier's
            mother, that I look out the window
want to write blue, want to defend
            the bones of tree branch
that skeleton the sky

BLACK ICE

A car drives
    into the cold dark.
        The mother, the son

a road through hills
    and music like a lake
        to skate across

cutting melody
    on the surface.
        There's no talk, the night

careens. They are out of sentences.
    They don't care. She pretends
        they are Gould's hands

shaping notes
    into sound
        across white

and black keys
    carving figure eights
        the hiss of blades.

AMERICAN MOTHER

There was the time I told your cradle I was done

Locked you in the van then shopped at Walgreens

I didn't feed you vegetables

I let the car slide into the lake, watched you drown and blamed Medea

I held each of you one by one under the porcelain water

Dozed as a man who wasn't your father broke your arm

I slapped your faces when your grades failed

When you were arrested I denied you were mine

I confess to being the mother of all bombs

Sometimes I disdained you

I confess I am not good

Sometimes the sound of the hawk

Chasing after the crow was the only thing I cared about

But I learned the word fontanel

Buried my face in the soft spot and oh the smell

The world of your skin the first morning after the night of your birth

Even the landscape of the heel of your day-old foot

The day gone to sleep and breast—your mouth opening

Then closing as if to tell me the story of what you saw—light

Glinting off a window and into your face—my

Large face like the ocean you would later swim in

Even as I love you and hold all of you

My children I'm the good mother the bad mother

The one who makes you

Then bombs your world to bits

BIRDS GATHER ON EMPTY GROUND

They splatter the sky with blue
and crimson, a troop of color

perched on a phone line
along the rutted road where I run

Sun Tzu says these are signs
Later I will read them

IV

DRONE MOTHER

For Jani Bergdahl, mother of Sergeant Bowe Bergdahl

I watch your father's hair and beard
      lengthen, spreading out the front door
as he tracks a fox
      across stream and meadow
He disappears for days
      We are become like animals

Falconoid
      I unravel the blue hidden in cirrus
thread the Hindu Kush
      Or I am the lark
you remembered from home
      the almostness of you

FIELD NOTES FROM HOME

OLGA

When he's home she dreams about teeth
—lined up in a cabinet like polished cubes
her English breaking down

as she describes the pool hall
on the base where she met
her husband an American

When he's gone she dreams
about the grinding jaw of a dog
which is what her mother in Kyrgyzstan

calls the husband though they talk
less and less and the streets
of Bishkek are fading

When he's home—maybe six weeks
in the two years of their marriage
she says she dreams of a house

at the edge of a cliff
It's dangerous and beautiful
Flocks of blue birds flank the bluff

She looking out a window
opens her mouth to take
a bite of the dog's face

SHARON

First deployment. Sharon watches the news.

Then on TV that roadside bomb exploded
in Iraq. Couldn't get hold of him.

Doesn't watch anymore. Too much.

After, they both jumped

at loud sounds like thunder or alarms.

Sorry about the house. No time to vacuum.

MARY

After he graduated from Basic

Mary says she flew home from Fort Benning

Goodbye to the tired Chattahoochee. The gaudy Spanish moss

All that ornamentation. Tattoo parlors and pawnshops

Old stucco buildings. Bad barbecue

She wanted to sleep, to never wake up

Then he was in Germany

Then Afghanistan

They couldn't Skype

He'd worry if he saw her face

Mary says these things at Starbucks

The machines hissing in the background

Some days she still feels like her whole body is burning

MADISON

My father was in Kuwait the day I was born

is what my mother says. Afghanistan

when I said my first words. I love running.

On cold clear mornings I hear the road breathing.

His face comes to me in the middle of a song.

Before things went bad, I remember he

would spin me. Whirring we went.

Our arms were spokes and trees streaked

by like brushstrokes against the backyard.

Mostly it's blurry. Sounds I remember.

Him singing loudly to heavy

metal music. Yelling at my mom.

Pacing around the house at night.

I don't see him much.

When we visit him in prison

we play Pictionary and Jenga.

He lets my little brother win.

KEVLAR POEM II

In dreams I'm the warrior
thrusting myself at traffic
Come morning the hunt

is mundane; nothing nips
at my heels. It's
out the door into the wild

suburban frontier
Who's fooling who
Survival here isn't

about dodging bombs
but which organic
vegetable should grace

the dinner table
In dreams
I'm protector of children

and for each trip
to the underworld
I slip on my Kevlar

its stronger-than-steel
filaments a shield
against the ordinary

SOLDIER UNDATED WORLD WAR I

His brow a bushy
     archipelago
Hands at parade rest
     Long fingers
and brass buttons hold steady along
     the front line of his uniform
There's restraint in his posture
     from boot to belt to chevron
until he's the story I was told
     My grandfather painting watercolors in France
battlefield fading to strokes
     of goldenrod light washed over the distant hills

RULES OF ENGAGEMENT

I decide to study the experts—Sun Tzu. Homer and Thucydides. Clausewitz. I learn warriors' rage is an essential storyline. And that war has no constant dynamic. Wound is the Greek word for trauma. Trauma stems from twisting or piercing. I resolve to surround my body with a great shield of books. Dickinson and Woolf and Rich. Reading and comprehension do not ease fear. I want to understand, *the thing itself*.

THE MAP IS NOT THE TERRITORY

The city isn't to be confused with the words that describe it, says Calvino. I read my mother's letters. Blue ink on onionskin paper. Palimpsest of her hand. Ghost image of her voice. Her younger self a house constructed of twigs and tumors that I suspend over my desk. It's not my map or hers. It's too late to describe that story. What to do with report cards and notebooks. CDs on a shelf, sneakers on the floor. What file folder for my son.

COMING HOME

Once the ruby ring flew across the African desert and over the Himalayas all the way to China. My father-in-law says he wore it for luck. He's resting between leg lifts at physical therapy. The ring rubbed against his machine gun as the bomber dove to break bridges apart. The plane flying over wide Burmese rivers that reminded him of the Hudson. The ring glinting in India's monsoon nights. I wheel him to his room as he finishes the story again. How it slipped off his hand, into the Atlantic, the ring a drop of red on the surface. The soldier blinking in the glare of rolling waves that carried him home.

AS THETIS

At night walking the road I look at the moon
Moon I say to the moon
I am torn
The night is haloed in screen light
The moon leans closer
Breathes into a clash of trees
Go on the moon nods
Say more
It will get you nowhere

V

I am subject to many winds.

—C. D. WRIGHT

EVERYTHING IS EVERYWHERE

The weather's a metaphor
for disorder: April's snow showers
crash the computer
chant a requiem for sidewalks
but I miss mud season
its wild color
the naked glow of tree frogs
rising like a blue pharmacy
in the field
to sing all night

OBON

Because they said the eager
ghosts return once a year

because I was hungry for your body
I drew your name on the lantern

to call you back in some form
chanted syllables of the Lotus

Sutra, stared at the monk's shaved
head, the mouth that opened

then closed around each vowel
and consonant, hoping you'd show

up as a shape or sound
and someone said there was a bear

outside the dharma hall
but I figured the dead sparrow

on the path, the women at dinner
weren't your reincarnated selves.

I burned a message in the bonfire,
searched the flames, did not see your face.

I saved a bone chip
before throwing the handful

of ash at the waves
ash blown back on my arm.

TEA WITH THE VIET CONG SOLDIER'S WIFE

I was finished with war poetry
    but the soldier's late

as the chalky broth of bánh
    tráng fumes in a blue

bowl like a Matisse cutout.
    I try to use words like gloss

while the rice milk dries in round sheets
    on a bamboo screen.

Nearby the Mekong snakes
    its war-weary waters from Tibet

through Burma, Laos, Thailand
    Cambodia and Vietnam.

Every word is a translation
    though the wife says the soldier

might not return in time
    so there's tea and rice cake,

a photograph of her sons.
    I want to tell her about mine

in distant deserts
 but decide against the word glow

because in another poem the river
 will sweat into evening

nipa palm leaves cathedral the river
 and the night dragon rises on the tide.

STRAY DOG STORY

She's a get-it-done kind of person says Rosie
                    a hold-down-the-fort woman.
She's the good wife

gets dinner on the table, listens when he calls
                    a go-to gal
his since middle school when she wore glasses and he was a punk.

It's snowing as Rosie tells her story. I'm listening
                    with a winter mind
and looking at the flakes assembling on branches in formation

lining up like good children her three small my three grown.

When he's in Afghanistan she sticks to her guns
                    keeps the household humming.
It's lonely for him stuck in some forward operating base.

They Skyped and she got depressed. Getting it done
                    got hard and lonely.
I get that I say, as one flake sticks to the pane

like some flash-in-the-pan bit of beauty.

He finds a dog Rosie explains and he's in
                    for the whole nine yards.
He loves the mutt, sleeps with it, gives that pup his all in all.

While Rosie's driving to doctor this and overdue bills that.
                                   There are responsibilities and
she knows she can't go off half-cocked.

The dog gets in heat, gets to be a pain
                                   fools around with bomb dogs.
What comes next is nothing she could fix—she's not that kind of
   fixer-upper.

The big guns shoot the dog there and then.
                                   When he Skypes he cries.

Words are empty Rosie explains.
                                   The snow charges hard.
She says words aren't enough are they ever I ask.

NOT THE SAME

after he was never himself he moved out met someone online
    crashed the car
went through our bank accounts we hardly talked he tried to get help
    but not
really what could I do there were the kids school his parents from
    Vietnam
against him serving when he died twenty-seven vets killed
    themselves
I think he reached the end Rosie explains

MEMORIAL

For Jason Lee, 26
from Fruitport
Michigan, killed
on patrol in Iraq
his slight smile
thumbnailed on screen
real as stone.
Kevin Hill, 23, of Brooklyn
slain at Contingency
Outpost Dehanna. Does his father
substitute dream for fact?
On his fourth tour, the waters
of Kandahar swallowed
Sgt. Trenton L. Rhea.
He glows like a prayer flag.
Click for Captain Victoria
Pinckney who died
when her KC-135 crashed
on a refueling mission to Afghanistan.
She's holding her infant son
the crook of her arm
missing from the world.

M16/M4

Firing your weapon is like discussing some big philosophical question over coffee in a café. I study Wikipedia. The M4 is replacing the M16. The soldier's friend posts an eleven-second video. Guns are fired. Clouds sweep over a line of men. Sunrays slice the billows in hyperbolic algorithms. Cardboard for practice. A piece of paper shivers near a boot. The bullets are real. The paper isn't the target. A machine beloved for its fatal qualities, writes Rimbaud.

ON THE SOLDIER'S BIRTHDAY

My son waits in line for mortar class. A good career move, he says. I
try to read Clausewitz again. Who warns there's no light of reason
on a battlefield. I google mortar explosions. Is picturing a crime of
imagination. The moon being nearly full, I watch it puddle on the
driveway as I walk the dog. An owl somewhere in the woods cries. My
son learns to set coordinates, call for mortar strikes. Danger may be
far off or nearby. He was small and almost perfect at birth. Did I raise
him up to be a warrior.

JALALABAD

Falling asleep I say the word Jalalabad. My tongue rolling over the syllables of the name of the city. The *aaa*s and *llll*s like bedtime prayers. The word a secret in my mouth that streams across lake through the night. Jalalabad says a coyote. I am late for everything because Jalalabad. I find it difficult to talk. In meetings, other words seem dissonant. Hours later I lose track in the canned goods aisle. By dinner, Jalalabad is an ancient desert city at the foot of the Khyber Pass, fed by rivers, with a highway from Kabul to Peshawar. It's a centerpiece on the kitchen table. It is orange and pomegranate. And soldiers near helicopters. I clean the sink. A sense of place is important to a reader. Jalalabad, sing my hands.

TRANSMIGRATION

Thousands upon thousands of soldier birds
ferry to the beat of wings
at the edge of your sleep
You watch them spiral
In unison they turn
wheeling beyond the moon
that scrapes at your window

POST SCRIPT

What else—
Their true names
That families still count the days
That I haven't traveled to Afghanistan
Soldiers deploy
My son still serves
That the long war goes on

NOTES

Nangarhar is a province in eastern Afghanistan on the border with Pakistan. It was once a refuge for Osama bin Laden. Its capital is the city of Jalalabad.

The hoopoe is a bird featured in the ancient Persian epic by Farid Attar, *The Conference of the Birds*.

A landay is a form of Pashtun folk poetry. The word means "short, poisonous snake." It is a primarily oral tradition that features couplets usually composed anonymously by women.

War reporters James Foley and Steven Soloff as well as aid worker David Haines, among others, were executed by ISIS.

Mohamedou Ould Slahi, a citizen of Mauritania, was detained at the detention camp in Guantánamo Bay, Cuba, from 2002 to 2016 without being charged with a crime. His journals, kept during his imprisonment, were published as *Guantánamo Diary* in 2015 by Little, Brown and Company.

Kevlar, a lightweight fiber that's stronger than steel, was invented in 1965 by Stephanie Kwolek (1923–2014), a scientist with DuPont.

Paula Loyd, a thirty-six-year-old researcher with a US Army Human Terrain System, was doused with gasoline and lit on fire in November 2008 while serving in Afghanistan. Loyd died from her injuries in January 2009 at Brooke Army Medical Center in San Antonio, Texas.

Army Private Bowe Bergdahl was captured by the Taliban in 2009 and held captive for five years after walking off his base in Afghanistan. He was released in 2014. Bergdahl was dishonorably discharged and demoted from sergeant to private in November 2017.

Marine Private Jonathan Lee Gifford, 30, was killed in Nasiriyah, Iraq, in 2003, two days after the start of the Iraq War. Army Corporal Jason Lee, 26, was killed in Baquba, Iraq, in 2007. Army Specialist Kevin Hill, 23, was killed in Afghanistan in 2009. Army Sergeant First Class Trenton L. Rhea, 33, died in 2013 in Kandahar, Afghanistan. Air Force Captain Victoria Pinckney, 27, died when her KC-135, which was supporting military operations in Afghanistan, crashed about 100 miles west of a US air base in Kyrgyzstan.

A variety of authors inspired me during the writing of this book. Quotations are from the following authors and their books: Italo Calvino's *Invisible Cities*, translated by William Weaver (Harcourt, 1974); Kevin Powers's *Letters Composed During a Lull in the Fighting* (Little, Brown 2014); Arthur Rimbaud's *Illuminations*, translated by John Ashbery (Norton, 2011); Sun Tzu's *The Art of War*, translated by John Minford (Penguin Classics, 2003); C.D. Wright's *Cooling Time: An American Poetry Vigil* (Copper Canyon, 2005).

This book is not a work of journalism, and to that end, some names and identities have been changed. I am especially grateful to the American Red Cross Greater New York Region's support group for military families. In particular I thank all the family members who generously shared their experiences with me in the course of my research. Additionally, I have been honored to serve as mentor and poetry editor for the Afghan Women's Writing Project, an online journal featuring poetry and essays by Afghan women, and to have conducted their online workshops with Afghan women writing in English.

I am also grateful to a number of friends, poets, and readers, all of whom have been with me as this book came into creation. To my poet teachers and friends Kate Knapp Johnson and Kathleen Ossip for their wise editorial guidance. Thank you to Marilyn Johnson and Louise Yelin of the SUNY Purchase College Writers Center for the time and space to begin this book. Thank you Rowan Ricardo Phillips for selecting my manuscript, and much gratitude to Sarah Gorham at Sarabande Books for her insights on its structure and stories. Thanks to the National Endowment for the Arts for believing the experiences of military families were worthy of a creative writing fellowship. To my dear friend Nancy Doyle Palmer, who gave me the gift of a room and time and the ocean. To Masha Hamilton, for founding the Afghan Women's Writing Project and for encouraging my writing. Thanks as well to Fran Richey for her faith in this project. To Ellen Williams for her willingness to read over the years. Finally, I am deeply grateful to my children and husband. Their patience, belief, and love sustained me throughout the writing of this book and beyond.

ACKNOWLEDGMENTS

Thank you to the editors of the following journals, which published these poems, sometimes in different versions and with different titles.

Bellevue Literary Review: "War Stories"
BigCityLit: "Obon"
Cherry Tree: "Landay"
Cider Press Review: "Flynn's Pond"
Drunken Boat: "Transmigration"
Heron Tree Review: "At the Shooting Range"
Sierra Nevada Review: "Drone Song," "Over Nangarhar"
Southern Humanities Review, Finalist, 2015 Auburn Witness Poetry Prize Honoring Jake Adam York: "On the Orange Jumpsuit"
Truck: "Praise Song"
Upstreet: "Globe Skimmer"
Utter: "The Matins Project"
Nothing To Declare: A Guide to the Flash Sequence (White Pine Press, 2016): "Cities & Signs & War," "Code Talk," "Contour Drawing," "Land Navigation," "M16/M4," "On the Soldier's Birthday," "Rules of Engagement," "The Map Is Not the Territory"
O-Dark-Thirty: "In the Red Cross Parking Lot after a Meeting on PTSD"

STEVE RAGO

PAMELA HART is writer-in-residence at the Katonah Museum of Art where she manages and teaches an arts-in-education program. She received the Brian Turner Literary Arts Prize in poetry in 2016. She was awarded a National Endowment for the Arts poetry fellowship as well as a fellowship from the SUNY Purchase College Writers Center. Toadlily Press published her chapbook, *The End of the Body*. She teaches at the Hudson Valley Writers' Center and is a visiting artist in the schools in Westchester County, New York. She is a poetry editor for the Afghan Women's Writing Project and for *As You Were: The Military Review*.

SARABANDE BOOKS is a nonprofit literary press located in Louisville, KY. Founded in 1994 to champion poetry, short fiction, and essay, we are committed to creating lasting editions that honor exceptional writing. For more information, please visit sarabandebooks.org.